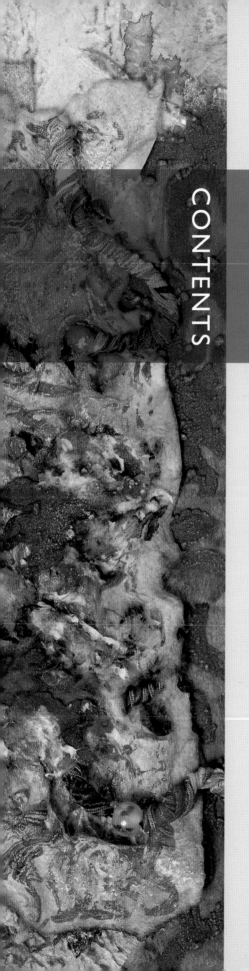

C000183004

CONTENTS

Materials

Water-soluble materials are incredibly versatile and this book aims to show how they can be used alone, employed as a support for other materials or layered over exciting surfaces to make a rich composition. Both water-soluble film and soluble paper offer innovative mixed media solutions. In addition to the use of dissolvable media, the book looks at extended techniques involving embossing powder, fine metal shim and kozo fibres.

Many forms of water-soluble media are available and they all work well. If you already have some, don't buy new but see how what you have works out. For most of the techniques, a fairly heavyweight film (such as the widely available Romeo) is suggested, but if you only have thin film, just use two layers. If you are seeking three-dimensional effects, a special 'Super' weight film is suggested but very little is needed and all scrap pieces can be recycled.

The other staple material is water-soluble paper. This is used in the book for mixed media effects in addition to its supporting role as a dissolvable. The papery effects achieved when it is used as paper pulp offer exciting surfaces, especially when dyed, painted or rusted.

< *This piece was made by couching bead chains and wrapped cords to water-soluble film. It would make a stunning piece of jewellery or could be used as an inset for a bag or decorative panel.*

Other materials included in these techniques can often be replaced by the recycled variety: metal shim makes a great surface for layers of water-soluble stitching but purée tubes or drinks cans may be substituted. Embossing powders and florists' wire are needed for some techniques but most of the remaining requirements will be found in the stash. Black plastic rubbish sacks make great cuffs and bags but do not involve a huge outlay.

So approach this book with an attitude of 'I'll use what I've got', rather than hitting the shops. Look out for all that stuff from the stitching shows, those left-over balls of knitting wool and that weird hairy yarn (you knew it would be useful one day) – and just have fun.

> *This sampler, demonstrating many of the techniques in the book, was made as a front panel for a bag. You can see the use of beaded chains with straight stitch fringing on an embossing powder surface with deeply embossed tiles.*

∨ *The use of wrapped cords and fringing techniques on water-soluble film produced this dramatic fragment ready to be attached to an embroidery.*

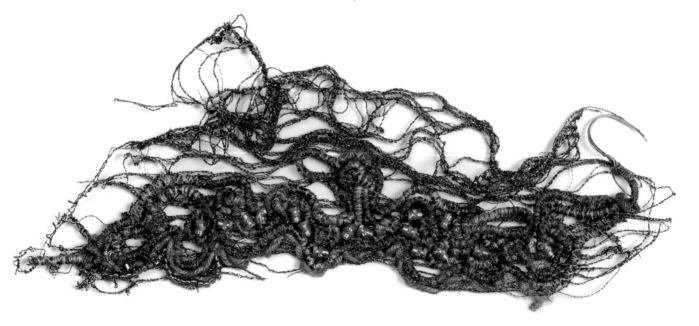

SECTION 1:
Encrusted Surfaces

This section of the book looks at the many surfaces that can be produced using only soluble film. It makes a fantastic base for richly embellished surfaces created by hand or machine stitching, and the following techniques show methods for producing pieces suitable for jewellery, panels, bags, book covers and vessels.

Basic method for encrusted surfaces

Bear in mind the ethos of using what you've got. If you can't get florists' wire, use any handy wire that can be bent easily. This could add a metallic element that might be fun.

∧ *The embellished strip can be used as a bracelet. .*

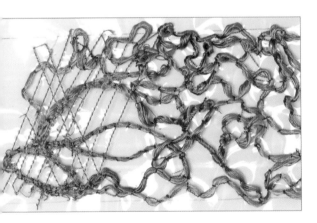

∧ *Here you can see the silk yarns used as the base, couched onto the dissolvable film.*

You'll need:
- water-soluble film that is thick enough to take hand and machine stitching
- knitting yarn or heavy embroidery thread
- florists' wire or similar
- beads, charms – anything attachable.

If you haven't got thick film, use two or three layers of thinner film. Solusheet or any of the dissolvable fabrics would also be fine.

Let's start with an embellished strip that can be used as a bracelet or cuff. It could easily be adapted to grow into a belt or a bag.

∨ *The threads wrapped on card are the ones used to make this bangle. Metallic thread, heavy silk yarn, novelty knitting yarn, cotton floss and dyed florists' wire.*

Stitching

1. On the film, mark a rectangular strip about 8 in. (20 cm) long. It doesn't matter what you use to draw the lines but avoid anything too inky as it may colour the piece when dissolved. I use a ballpoint pen. Frame up the film if hand stitching.

2. Take some weighty embroidery or knitting yarn and stitch it to the film, keeping within the marked area. This could be stitched in a formal design of squares, lines that cross each other or straight lines that run horizontally with the odd vertical line crossing them. The yarns could also meander in a free and easy flowing design. They could also be couched by hand or machine.

3. With the base yarns in place, you now need to machine stitch over the top using the normal sewing foot and straight stitches: stitch over the yarn as well. Although the general rule when machining water-soluble materials is to go over each line of stitching twice, this is not necessary when using straight stitch with the feed dogs up. *Do not dissolve it yet.*

> **NOTE:** Steps 2 and 3 can be reversed by machine stitching first, but I find that machining after hand stitching gives a firmer base.

4. Paint or dye the florists' wire and allow it to dry. Silk paints are good as they do not run when you dissolve the film (use a heat tool to set the colour). Hand or machine stitch the wire around the edges of the stitched strip to add stability. Add further florists' wire, yarn or thread to fill the empty areas and include a metallic thread such as jap gold for a little gleam. This is useful to integrate multi-coloured areas.

These four steps make a framework to build on. They form a base for your encrusted surface. Now the fun can begin. Gather up a selection of goodies to stitch on top. Consider:

- beads – all kinds, either themed or totally random
- shells and charms – anything that can be attached by stitching
- coloured wire, twisted into curly shapes
- pearl purl (a goldwork wire that can be slightly stretched and will add stability)
- hand stitching – you won't need a frame as the surface will be quite firm.

Now you can see why the film was not dissolved before. It is so much easier to work into with the film in place. You must be sure to stitch into the yarn or straight stitches. If stitched into the film, the bead or charm will fall off when the film is dissolved.

Dissolving

When you are quite sure that you have finished decorating the film and it is suitably encrusted (remember the edges: do they need beading?), cut away all the excess film and save it for another project. Pin the stitched strip carefully to a piece of polystyrene, using lots of pins, before holding it under lukewarm running water. If stubborn, soak for a while.

A general rule about dissolving: check to make sure that all surfaces are joined by stitch. Remember that the film will not be there to hold things together, so anything not joined to its neighbour will float away.

Extension technique

Don't overlook the charm of basic hand stitches. Try swirls or circles of running stitch (stitch before beading) or lines of raised chain band with beads weaving in and out. Narrow ribbons, especially the wired variety, fit in well with today's look for cuffs and belts. Don't be afraid to experiment. Couched threads (try those hairy ones) also work well and could be attached with decorative stitching.

< The bag was made from silk and wool fibres, dry felted using an embellisher machine. The encrusted surface forms the centre panel.

Machine stitching

Work, as before, to the end of step 3. Then add machine stitching to the mix. Try one or all of the following ideas. Remember not to cover the film completely as some 'holes' add a lacy effect.

- Couch down more heavy threads by machine (try twisting them first for extra interest).
- Built-in patterns (some of the chunky satin stitch type) can work well. If your machine has no built-in patterns then put the film in a frame and set up for free machining. Work your widest zigzag while gently pulling the frame from side to side to achieve a scalloped effect. If working satin stitch patterns, secure them with a straight stitch down the centre of the pattern to prevent unravelling. Some patterns will only partially undo, making an interesting texture. Experiment and keep a note of which stitch works and which doesn't. The lines of stitch can be beaded, too.
- Machine-wrap the florists' wire by working a narrow satin stitch over the top. This gives a different effect to the painted wire while still being useful for structure.
- Add hand stitching to the machining; needle weaving techniques work especially well.

∨ A detail of the finished piece. Note the combination of hand and machine stitching.

Extension technique

Make a narrow panel, as shown, to form the centre of a small bag. The background to this one was made using the embellisher machine but it could also be formed from any of your favourite backgrounds. I used a base of black felt with shades of grey wool tops. Hand stitching formed a border motif and was then embellished. The water-soluble panel was mounted over a scrap of silver fabric and was hand stitched firmly around the edge but very lightly in the centre. This gives great depth to the encrusted yarn centrepiece.

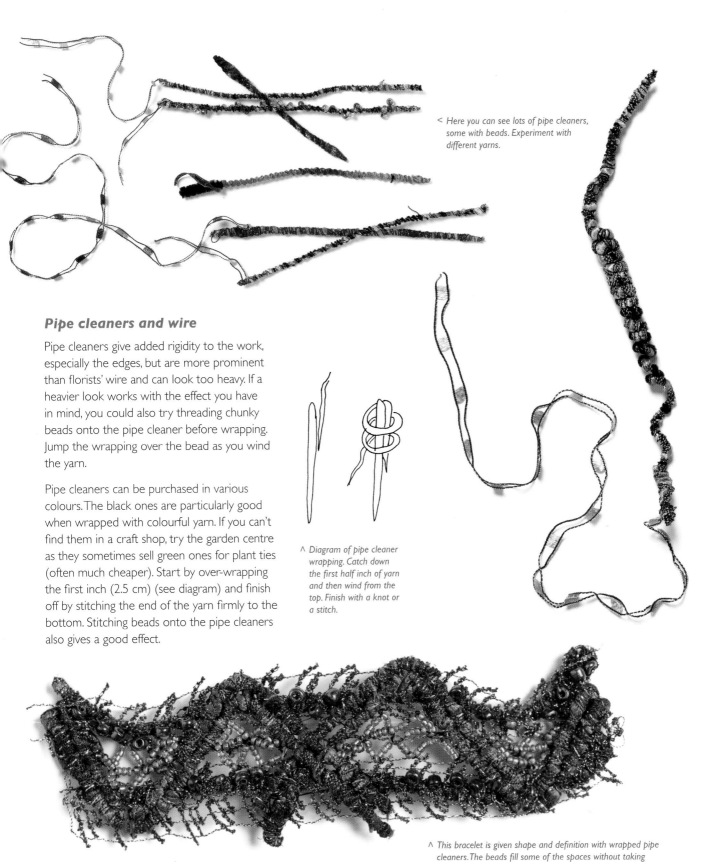

< Here you can see lots of pipe cleaners, some with beads. Experiment with different yarns.

Pipe cleaners and wire

Pipe cleaners give added rigidity to the work, especially the edges, but are more prominent than florists' wire and can look too heavy. If a heavier look works with the effect you have in mind, you could also try threading chunky beads onto the pipe cleaner before wrapping. Jump the wrapping over the bead as you wind the yarn.

Pipe cleaners can be purchased in various colours. The black ones are particularly good when wrapped with colourful yarn. If you can't find them in a craft shop, try the garden centre as they sometimes sell green ones for plant ties (often much cheaper). Start by over-wrapping the first inch (2.5 cm) (see diagram) and finish off by stitching the end of the yarn firmly to the bottom. Stitching beads onto the pipe cleaners also gives a good effect.

∧ Diagram of pipe cleaner wrapping. Catch down the first half inch of yarn and then wind from the top. Finish with a knot or a stitch.

∧ This bracelet is given shape and definition with wrapped pipe cleaners. The beads fill some of the spaces without taking over the shape.

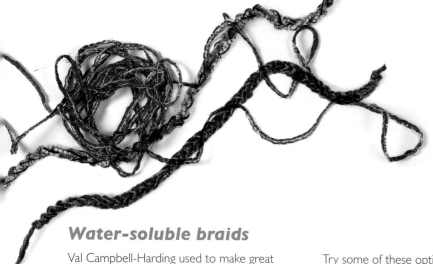

> The braids are easily made by laying yarns and metallic thread on water-soluble film. Then use a narrow zigzag stitch to join them together. Place the next one up close to save wasting film.

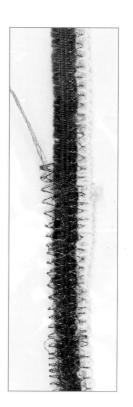

Water-soluble braids

Val Campbell-Harding used to make great braids by stitching a pattern over several thick threads at once. For this, you need a machine with a 9mm stitch width. If the same operation is performed with the yarns or threads placed on water-soluble film, it is much easier and a narrow zigzag can be used, just joining up two threads at the same time. Simply lay two side by side and stitch (normal stitching, feed dogs up). Add another one, perhaps a gold or silver thread, and stitch again. Remember that the top machine thread will show, so choose a suitable colour or a metallic one.

Try some of these options:
- use built-in patterns instead of zigzag
- make wide strips and narrow strips
- plan a colour scheme and work the threads accordingly
- add machine-wrapped florists' wire to make the braids 'bendable'.

I made a book cover from the braids by taking colour inspiration from a pack of Mulberry Silks threads. Braids were then made as above, by laying the threads next to each other on water-soluble film, leaving some gaps for hand stitching. After working hand stitches and securing with a line or two of machine stitching across the diagonal to prevent unravelling (remember the rules about dissolving), the film was dissolved and placed over metal shim for a book cover.

∨ This book cover was made from colour-schemed braids, joined by hand stitching.

∨ The colour scheme for this piece of work was taken from a pack of Mulberry Silks threads.

Raising the surface

Having had fun with the couching and braiding techniques, it is time to start raising the surface of the stitching and adding some glamour with beads and rich metallic cords.

Beaded chains

Beaded chains (see diagram below) look great nestling into the surface and can be used with the cuffs and bracelets shown or added to the braids by stitching on top of the braid. Secure the chains to the base stitching and make sure they are well supported before dissolving. Alternatively, work bead chains directly into the couched soluble film by anchoring the beading yarn into the basic lines of stitching, before working the chain.

If you are a keen beader, you could also consider using bead weaving techniques. If not, how about looking for some ready-strung ropes of freshwater pearls.

∨ *Beaded chains and hand stitching.*

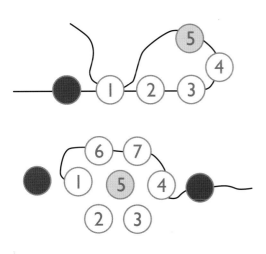

∧ *A diagram for a simple beaded flower chain. Thread on three beads for the base between flowers, then four in the flower colour and one contrast bead. Go back through the first bead in the flower, pick up two more beads and then exit through bead four.*

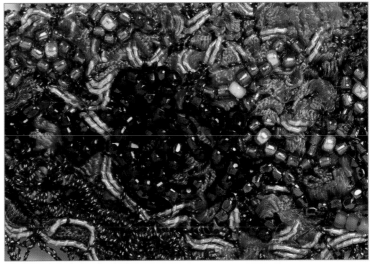

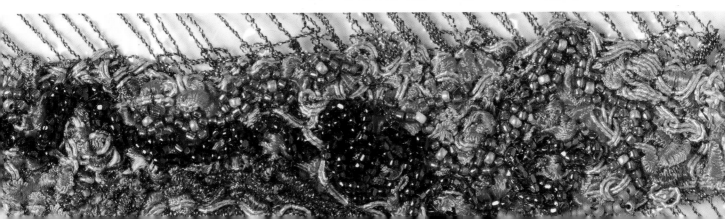

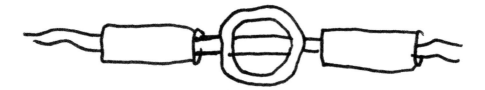

Wrapped cords

Machine-wrapped cords have so many uses and can add a distinctive sense of weight to an encrusted water-soluble film surface. They work well with all the techniques described previously. If a metallic thread is used on the bobbin, a wonderful sparkle lifts the work. So try using wrapped cords with the beads and stitching described on the previous pages. Here's the basic method, if you haven't tried making these cords before.

1. Take string or several lengths of weighty yarn as base cords. String gives a stiff finish that's great for belts and jewellery. Use a special foot with a tunnel underneath, if possible, or try using your darning (embroidery) foot and taping short lengths of drinking straw in front of and behind the needle to guide the threads through (see diagram above). This will stop the cord threads bouncing about while you are covering them.

2. Set the machine to the widest zigzag and feed the base cords through the tunnel under the foot. Use your left hand to hold them behind the machine. Start to stitch, keeping a slight tension on the threads behind the needle. Don't pull too hard: just keep the threads running through smoothly.

3. Tie off the ends of the threads and secure with a tiny dab of glue or a stitch or two.

The original base cords that were wrapped can also be used to add to the effect. If you wrap thinly, the base colour will show through. If you stitch heavily, you can completely cover

∧ *A piece of drinking straw can be taped in front of, and behind, the darning foot. This keeps the yarn to be wrapped running straight.*

the threads and make a thicker cord. Using textured knitting threads gives a knobbly effect.

The cords produced using this method have a lovely texture and are excellent just as they are for ties around embroidered book covers, plaited or wound together for bag handles, linked in a more chunky fashion for belts, or stitched down onto fabric for a raised textured effect. Make several cords in colours that work well together.

Here's how to use wrapped cords for a bracelet with soluble film:

1. Mark the size required on the dissolvable film (make sure that you use a firm one) and proceed as before, stitching a base on which to attach the cords. Make sure that the yarn and the thread used for stitching are close in colour to the wrapped cords.

2. Now stitch the cords to the base fabric, making sure that they are securely attached. They could be stitched in a formal pattern such as loops, circles or swirls or just allowed to wander. They can be stitched to the base by hand or machine. Add beads, especially flower chains, as described earlier.

3. Pin out and dissolve as before.

∧ *Finished cord piece showing a close-up of the cords and flower chains.*

Extension technique

A really chunky alternative is to knot several cords together before attaching, perhaps varying the colours. When attaching knots, take several stitches on each side of the knot, plus one or two through the knot itself, making sure that you stitch into the base stitching. If you prefer to machine stitch, don't try to stitch over the knots; just secure by hand afterwards.

Adding knotted cords to the basic technique certainly provides the wow factor. Great for both chunky cuffs and narrow bracelets, it also makes statement necklaces – imagine a 'torc' style as in the drawing: fabulous.

∨ *This drawing of a torc-style necklace shows how wrapped cords would work well for other pieces of adornment.*

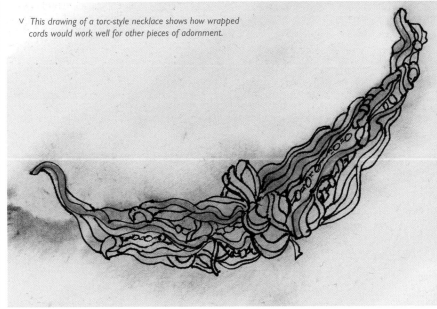

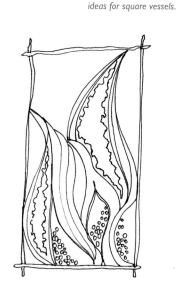

> Beaded flower chains can be dipped
into melted embossing powders. Bear in
mind that this stiffens them and is not
suitable for a draped effect.

Cords with beads

Here are some exciting ways to add sparkle to
cords using beads.

- When stitching the cords to the background,
  leave gaps between them and then fill them
  with tiny beads. Large beads, in the same
  colourway, can be stitched along the edge of
  the piece. Remember to anchor the beads
  firmly to the base stitching.
- Taking one of the machine threads that had
  been used to wrap the cords, thread beads
  down its length. Secure the end so that they
  don't fall off. Hand-wrap the cords with the
  beaded thread, moving the beads down, one
  at a time, so that they are spaced regularly.
  Stitch into the cord to finish off, then knot
  and apply as before.
- Thread the beads as before and add them
  to the cord as it is wrapped by the sewing
  machine. Separate the beads as you work
  down, wrapping the base and covering the
  bead thread at the same time. Be careful not
  to hit the beads or you may break a needle.
  They do usually seem to slide out of the way.

Make beaded chains
(see page 9 for a flower
chain) and stitch these
to the base fabric, making
sure they are well supported.
They look wonderful nestled into
the cords. If you find the beaded
chains too precise, dab them with a little
acrylic paint and immediately sprinkle with
embossing powder. Do this over a piece of
paper and you can catch the excess powder
by giving the chain a shake. Now lay on baking
paper and melt the powder with a heat tool.
When cool, you can stitch it down as before.
Don't add too much powder or it may come
off – a little goes a long way.

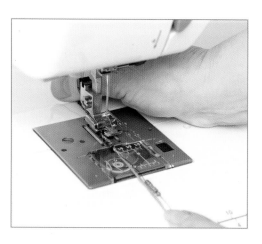

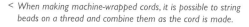

v Mixing cords with
stitched areas gives
sufficient stability for
three-dimensional work.
Here are some design
ideas for square vessels.

< When making machine-wrapped cords, it is possible to string
beads on a thread and combine them as the cord is made.

< *Square-sided vessel with dissolved stitching on Romeo film. The sides were made from moulding strips from a DIY store and the embellishment is wrapped pipe cleaners which add rigidity to the stitching.*

Painted cords

In our spirit of making the most of what we have, a great idea is to wrap cords using up all your old machine threads and then paint them with metallic paint. This works best with dark-coloured threads or cords that have previously been painted with a darkish paint. It's best to complete all the stitching and dissolving before painting and then to allow the item to dry. Place on baking paper and use a dry brush of gold, copper or silver acrylic, gradually adding layers and drying the piece in between. If beads are part of the piece, try painting those too. A little embossing powder could be sprinkled onto the tacky acrylic – endless possibilities.

∨ *The red cords were too bright and overpowering so they were painted in a darker colour. This is a good method for using up old threads and some interesting space-dyed effects can be achieved when a pale colour is dipped in water first and then painted with several colours.*

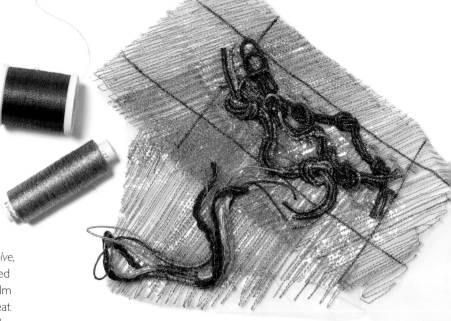

Massed lines of stitch

I discovered in a previous book, *Stitch, Dissolve, Distort*, published by BT Batsford, that massed lines of straight stitching on water-soluble film give a terrific effect when dissolved, and great new techniques have led from this approach. Here's a recap on the basic method.

1. Draw a rectangle about 5 x 3 in. (12.5 x 7.5 cm) with a ballpoint pen. If you use firm film, there is no need for an embroidery frame for the stitching.

2. Stitch with the feed dogs up using the ordinary sewing foot. The bobbin thread will show, so check the colour. Work diagonal lines as shown above.

   Continue to stitch diagonal lines, very close to each other, over the whole of the rectangle. You don't need to stitch twice over the lines and it doesn't matter if they wobble a bit or cross each other here and there. Do stitch lots of lines – it is a bit boring, but necessary.

3. This step is vital if the whole thing isn't to unravel at the dissolving stage. Stitch a smaller rectangle about 2 or 3 in. (5 cm) in from the edges to anchor the lines. Stitch lines from the corners too, to avoid the unsecured lines being washed away.

4. *Inside* this rectangle, work some machine patterns or hand stitches in the same way as the basic technique. Lots of knotted, wrapped cords, beads and/or beaded chains work well, too. Don't add anything outside the narrow central strip.

5. Cut away all excess film and pin the main area onto polystyrene. Dissolve carefully, leaving behind a small quantity of the water-soluble film – not enough to feel sticky but just enough to stiffen a little bit.

6. When dissolved, remove onto baking paper and prod the fringes into waves and curls. Allow to dry.

Your piece should have wonderful, curled-up fringes. Add a fastener to make a bracelet.

∧ *Masses of straight lines were worked on water-soluble film using metallic thread on top and in the bobbin. In this photo, you can see the wrapped cords which were knotted and secured inside the central rectangle of stitching.*

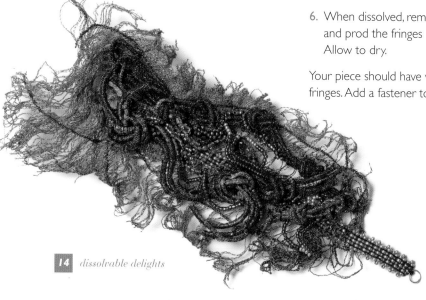

< *The finished cuff after dissolving. Wrapped cords and flower chains were hand stitched to the massed straight lines and a very small amount of the film was allowed to remain to help with the shape.*

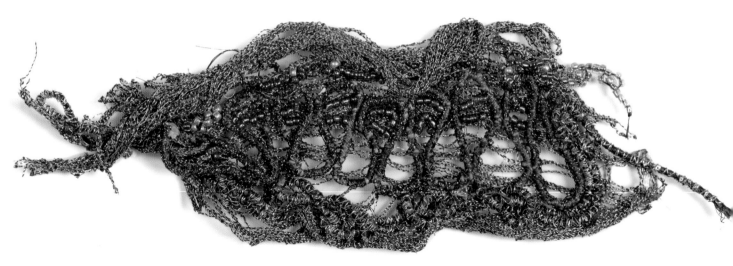

∧ Cords add definition to the centre of this bracelet.

Extension technique

Use your curly piece as the central panel of a bag. The one shown here was made, using the embellisher machine, from felt and silk fibres. A little black chiffon added definition. Here's the method:

1. Cut two pieces of black felt, a little bigger than the size required.

2. Use the embellisher to add colourful silk fibres, merge them and swirl them for a marbled effect.

3. Lay a dark-coloured chiffon scarf on top. Make sure that this is bigger than the bag shape. Now embellish the chiffon over the silks, starting in the middle and following the marbled swirls. Allow the chiffon to bunch and add dark streaks and lines to the marbled effect.

4. Trim the edges and lay the front on the back, right side out. Embellish the sides to attach front to back.

5. Use the curly fringes to accentuate an embellishment, such as the piece of cast paper shown here.

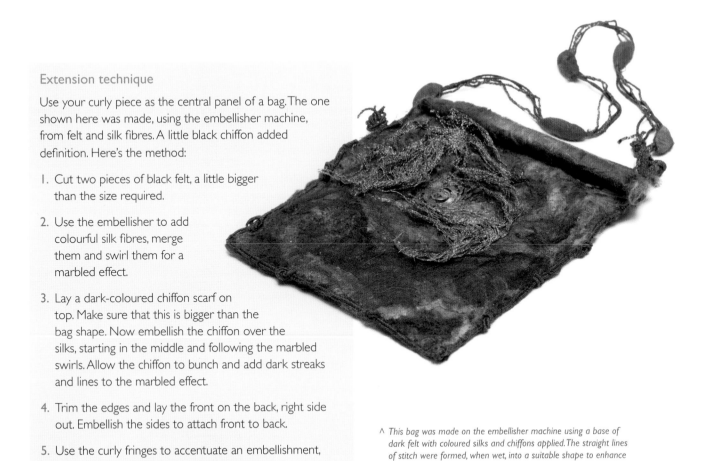

∧ This bag was made on the embellisher machine using a base of dark felt with coloured silks and chiffons applied. The straight lines of stitch were formed, when wet, into a suitable shape to enhance a water-soluble paper motif (page 32). When dissolved, the gold stitching was very firm but was still easy to apply with hand stitching.

Soluble film for three-dimensional effects

There is a specific make of soluble film that is wonderful for three-dimensional effects and jewellery. It is made by The Soluble Film Company and is called 'Super' weight. Much heavier than the usual film, it gives substance to the finished piece, especially if a very small amount of film remains after dissolving.

Although large pieces can be worked with the film and masks are particularly successful, I love to use it for brooches, pins and tiny boxes and vessels. The wrapped cords add extra weight here, especially when narrow cords are used to outline motifs.

Keep the motif reasonably simple as it will have to be outlined with the cords. The design shown here will give you an idea – many design books or even children's colouring books will have similar ones.

Here's how:

1. Place the 'Super' film over the design and draw in the main lines with a ballpoint pen. This won't run and spoil the thread colour.

2. Set the machine for free machining and put the film in a hoop – this is not strictly necessary but it helps with smaller designs.

3. Stitch the design using a filling stitch, such as very small circles. Run the machine fast and move the hoop slowly.

4. When the design area is filled, couch the narrow wrapped cords around the edge. I usually do this by hand as it is essential to catch the cord to the stitching and curves are much more accurate. If you have a simple design, by all means have a go at machining the cords down using a zigzag stitch. Match the thread to the cord colour.

5. Cut the stitching away from the film and hold under running warm water.

6. Leave some of the gooey film in the stitching to stiffen it. This may involve several re-washes – better to stop too soon than to wash it all out.

In this section we have covered most of the basic techniques using just the film. In the next section, we incorporate other materials and take a look at supported stitching.

∧ *Here you can see a stitched motif and two with cord stitched around the edges, ready for dissolving.*

∨ *Brooches made from this method and a square, suitable for applying to a background.*

∧ *Motif design.*

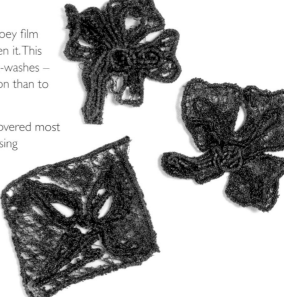

SECTION 2:
Building up the Surface

In this section, we'll be looking at the possibilities of extending some of the earlier methods and using the strength of the heavy water-soluble film as an overlay, as a base for some unique fringing effects or as a support for a variety of surfaces. The joy of dissolvable film is that it allows the use of layers of fabric without the density brought by more solid materials.

Overlays

It is possible to produce some interesting effects by using water-soluble strips or small motifs as a top layer, or overlay, over previously stitched surfaces. Especially effective if the stitching uses metallic thread, this layer will really stand out, whereas the same design will disappear into the fabric if simply stitched on top.

In the photograph, left, you can really see the difference. As you can imagine, this is also a good way to float a stitched surface onto materials like thick metal or polymer clay, which are not stitch friendly.

∧ The dissolved built-in patterns have been 'floated' over a base of carrier rods stitched to felt.

Built-in patterns

If your sewing machine offers you a range of built-in patterns, these can look very effective when used as an overlay. The satin stitch ones suggest exciting distressed metallic patterns when dissolved. Work like this:

1. Using a medium-weight soluble film, stitch rows using one of the heavier patterns with a metallic thread top and bottom.

2. Stitch a slightly larger area than you wish to cover and join the rows with straight lines of stitching, through the middle of the pattern. This will limit the erosion of the stitching when dissolved but still allow a degree of distortion.

3. Pin the stitching out on a polystyrene (pizza base) support and dissolve carefully. Soak it rather than holding under a tap.

4. When dry, attach to a suitable base fabric by catching here and there: hand stitch or use the machine by just adding a few straight stitches in places. Don't flatten it by machining heavily all over.

5. If floating the piece over clay or heavy metal, make it slightly larger and wrap around, using glue on the wrong side. Alternatively, make holes in the clay before baking and lace the overlay in place.

∨ *Auto patterns on film and dissolved, some allowed to unravel. These are great for adding texture to a stitched piece.*

> **NOTE:** Sometimes it is fun to omit the lines of straight stitching and let the patterns unravel a little. They can be couched onto a piece of fabric to give it a distressed effect, especially when a gold metallic is used for the top thread with a variegated metallic in the bobbin. I keep stores of these 'unravellings' and use them to couch down on top of a fabric background or trap them between sheer fabrics.

This is a fun technique and you might like to play with some of the following:
- Try a variegated thread on top and a metallic on the bobbin. Play with the tension for different effects.
- Free machine larger motifs and work auto patterns, or blobs, over the top of them.
- If your machine has a memory, experiment with combining different patterns, perhaps a scroll joining a flowery motif.
- Make patterns larger by free machining around the edges.

Satin stitch 'blobs'

If you don't have any patterns, try making 'blobs' of satin stitch by stitching heavily in one place, working to a grid. Set up the machine for normal sewing, feed dogs up, and select the widest zigzag and a very short length, so that the stitches close up on each other. Work bursts of stitches around a central point for a flower effect. When this has been achieved, select a narrow zigzag and stitch a stalk joining up with the next blob. For greater emphasis and bigger motifs, switch to machine embroidery and straight stitch around the motif. Join everything up by straight stitching over the top to hold it all together.

Fringes and edgings

One of the joys of water-soluble film is that it is heavy enough to support the placement of other fabrics on top, which makes it possible to add lovely lacy effects to the edges of them.

I am going to demonstrate this with a series of amulet bags, small enough to wear around the neck but with enough surface area to allow decoration. These were inspired by the little silk purses made by Carol Coleman. The edging method is the same for all of them, so it will only be described in full for the first purse. However, the body of the purse can be made from a variety of materials, either using your favourite techniques or trying those set out overleaf.

Metal shim amulet purse

An easy way of achieving good results with the purse is to place a suitable 'centre' on the film and then to stitch around the edges, giving a lacy finish to the sides and elongating the base into a luxurious fringe.

Starting with metal effects, you will need a small piece of shim or a cut-up tomato purée tube. If using shim, make sure that it is fine metal that can be stitched by machine. (Check with your supplier if you are unsure.) Work like this:

1. Cut out a piece of metal about 2½ × 1 in. (7 × 2.5 cm). Hold in a candle flame or use a paint stripper to colour it, if you wish. Mind your fingers on the sharp edges.

2. Draw into the metal with an embossing tool or an old ballpoint pen. Press hard and doodle away to make a pattern on the metal.

3. Apply dark acrylic paint on the metal and wipe it off with a kitchen towel. Don't wipe it all off – leave some paint in the depths of the inscribed lines. This gives an antique effect.

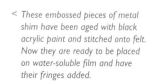

< These embossed pieces of metal shim have been aged with black acrylic paint and stitched onto felt. Now they are ready to be placed on water-soluble film and have their fringes added.

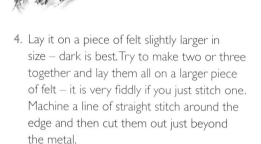

4. Lay it on a piece of felt slightly larger in size – dark is best. Try to make two or three together and lay them all on a larger piece of felt – it is very fiddly if you just stitch one. Machine a line of straight stitch around the edge and then cut them out just beyond the metal.

5. Using a heavy yarn, buttonhole around the edge by hand. This gives a surface to machine into in the next step.

6. Lay the pieces, one at a time, on heavy water-soluble film. Set up for free machine stitching and work a lacy edge around the top and sides of the bag, connecting with and covering the buttonhole stitch.

7. Work a straight stitch fringe on the bottom of the bag by stitching straight lines down, taking care to start each line in the felt. Then dissolve.

8. Make another metal and felt piece up to step 5 for the back of the bag. Cut it out and hand or machine stitch to the front. Complete with a wrapped cord or beaded chain.

These purses work really well with an overlay, made using one of the smaller built-in pattern stitches.

∧ Metal purses with water-soluble fringes.

Embossing powder purses

This technique gives an amazing, deeply etched, metal-like surface that is relatively easy to stitch and is based on embossing powder and felt. The method shown below is for people who do not have a Melting Pot – a dedicated, thermostatically controlled pan for melting embossing powder.

This is a wonderful way to make exciting metallic jewellery and always provokes 'how did you make that?' comments. I have made a little purse here but, in the final section, we will be using it for exciting mixed media techniques. Work on a tray to contain any 'blown about' powder.

Here's the basic method:

1. Cover the working surface and tray – this could get messy. Take a piece of baking paper and paint the central area with acrylic paint, any colour. The thickness of the paint is crucial and you may need a couple of attempts to get it right. It should not be so thick that you can see blobs of paint or so thin that the paper shows through.

2. Quickly, before the paint dries, sprinkle it thickly with ultra-thick embossing enamel (UTEE) powder. Shake off the excess powder onto some paper and shoot it back into the pot.

3. Place it on a heat-proof surface and heat it with a heat tool until it bubbles. Very quickly, while it is still hot, sprinkle more UTEE on it and heat it again. If the melted UTEE was too cold to hold more powder, just heat again until it bubbles. Work along the stripe of paint, heating it well as you go and shaking a very small amount of powder directly onto the gooey mass just heated. Turn the heat tool away while you do this so the powder does not blow away.

4. Allow the UTEE to cool a little so that you can examine it closely to make sure that all the paint is well covered and the UTEE is quite thick. If not, heat and add more powder. Peel off some of the UTEE strip and place, paint side down, on a strip of felt and heat until liquid.

5. Have a rubber stamp handy: moulding mats are brilliant for this. Then stamp into the hot powder, engraved side of stamp down. Be very careful not to touch the hot enamel. Press the stamp lightly and leave for a minute or so. Do not worry if the felt reacts to the heat.

6. When cool, remove the stamp. It should come away easily and leave a deeply incised surface that can be cut to shape with scissors.

^ Marbled UTEE stamped
 on felt.

This technique has so many uses, not only for the purses shown here but also for jewellery such as bracelets, necklaces, cuffs and earrings. The pieces can be cut to a shape and applied to panels or bags.

If you have a Melting Pot, just pour the UTEE onto the stamp and carefully, minding your fingers, press the felt into it, holding it down on each side of the stamp. Remove when cold.

Points to note when using UTEE with stamps:

- I have never had a problem with stamps sticking but it is probably best not to use your very best stamps for a first attempt.
- There should be no need to grease the rubber stamp.
- If it does stick, it will be because the acrylic paint was not fully covered. Do check to make sure.
- Speed is of the essence, so make sure that you have everything to hand – the UTEE, the paper and the stamp – before you start.
- Watch out – it gets very hot.
- Try using black UTEE for the first two layers and then add a little of the interference coloured powder – this gives a lovely marbled look.

< The use of black embossing enamel
 allows the interference powders to
 produce wonderful oil-slick colours
 as shown above.

< A flowery rubber stamp was used to press into the hot UTEE on felt. This was cut to size to make a small purse front.

Making the purse

To make an amulet purse using the inscribed UTEE, just cut two pieces from the stamped felt to the size required. Save the remainder of the UTEE-d felt as it will be used again later.

Draw the shape of the cut-out purse front on a piece of water-soluble film. Machine some firm threads into the film and around the edge of the drawn line.

Place the cut-out front on top and hand stitch it to the stitched threads. Buttonhole stitch is a good one to use. Go over the thread around the edge and then take the needle into the felt just below the UTEE.

It isn't possible to use the machine to attach the purse front to the film as the enamel sets so hard that the needle would break. However, now that it is attached firmly to the water-soluble film, it is possible to free machine a lacy edge and a curly bottom fringe as before, by stitching into the heavy yarn around the edges of the purse. If any neatening is needed, couch a skinny wrapped cord by hand all around the front. Dissolve the water-soluble film and hand stitch the back as before.

^ When the purse front is attached to the film, it can have a free machine edging and fringe stitched around it.

Extension technique

Cut shapes from the embossed felt and apply them to a background fabric, as shown in this piece. Here the shapes have been combined with a silk fabric. The metal strips have a 'floated' pattern, stitched on water-soluble film, attached.

^ This embossed purse has a strap made from one of the braids shown in Section 1.

< Sweetie papers and the papers on felt.

Sweetie paper purses

These are made by using Bondaweb (fusible webbing) to bond chocolate foil to felt. I always used to insist that it must be the proper foil, not the plastic or paper alternative, but I've since had great results with the plastic stuff. This can be painted with metallic paint or waxed, which must dry well before the next step. Tissue paper, with a drawing or stamped motif, is then ironed on top. Make a sizeable piece as it is less fiddly and the left-overs make great cards.

1. Iron a piece of fusible webbing (the same size as the sweetie paper) onto felt. Remove the paper and iron the sweetie paper over the top, protecting the surface with baking paper.

2. Use a stamp or ballpoint pen (in this case, trace or draw a design) to get a design onto fine tissue paper to fit the front of the purse – abaca tissue is good but ordinary tissue is fine, too.

3. Glue the tissue to the sweetie paper with a medium such as Ormaline or Sonja Jo. Even PVA will work if you add a little water to dilute it. Allow to dry thoroughly.

4. Add a little colour to the tissue with crayons, pastels or watercolours if you wish. For a whole book full of ideas on colouring a base like this, treat yourself to **Fabulous Surfaces** by Lynda Monk (see Suppliers at the end of this book). Dry thoroughly.

5. Stitching can be added now, but bear in mind that it might be too small and fiddly.

6. Paint with acrylic wax or a matt varnish to protect the surface. Then when dry, cut out and apply to water-soluble film as before.

∧ Two little sweetie paper purses, made using the tissue paper and acrylic medium method.

Supported surfaces

The ideas that follow show what can happen when film is combined with fabric. Most of the fabrics will be found in the stash: net, sheers, silk fibres and so on.

One that you might have to purchase is called trilobal nylon fibre, which looks unpromising at first glance but has lots of possibilities, as it reacts to heat.

Water-soluble film and sheer fabrics

The easiest way to start is just to trap strips of sheer fabric between two layers of water-soluble – clear film is best for this technique. The stitching should not be too delicate or it won't be able to compete with the different surfaces. Bold is best. Draw the design on the top layer with a ballpoint pen.

1. Cut two strips of film and lay one on the worktop. Cover with torn strips of sheer fabric, making sure that there are some gaps.

2. Place the top film, with the design, on top and check that the strips are well placed in relation to the design.

3. Frame up carefully, making sure that the strips don't move.

4. Work the design with hand or machine stitching. Try to make sure that the stitching catches in all the strips and that any stitching that is unsupported by fabric is secured with extra stitch.

5. Pin and dissolve as usual.

6. When dry, remove and examine the result, cutting away any fabric or tatty stitching, as necessary.

∧ 'Amphora' was made using the water-soluble sandwich method. After the design had been drawn on the film, some machining was used to stabilise the work. This firmed it up to support hand stitching.

> 'Agnes' by Jo Beattie features a water-soluble film sandwich, with the image drawn on the dissolvable fabric with wash-away felt-tip pen. Different-coloured nylon gauzes were sandwiched between the layers of dissolvable fabric. Then the design was machine embroidered. After the water-soluble material had been soaked away, some more of the coloured fabric was cut away.

Water-soluble film and net

Net responds really well to heavy stitching but water-soluble film is needed to support it. Even in a frame, it is difficult to prevent it from getting chewed up without adequate support. Another advantage is that a little of the film can remain at the washing-out stage so that a shape can be formed. Use the firmer net, sometimes called 'ballet net', and combine it with a metallic thread as well as a plain colour for some super results.

A really exciting effect can be obtained using the 'Super' weight film (see Suppliers). This makes the net really stiff, especially if a little of the film is allowed to remain after dissolving.

< 'This box was made from two layers of net supported by water-soluble film. Some of the 'Super' weight film was allowed to remain after dissolving to give a firm result.

∧ Net fascinators made
by supporting ballet
net with water-soluble
'Super' weight film. Flower
shapes were stitched
and moulded when wet.
Several of the flowers were
joined by stitching together
before stitching to a comb.

In the following instructions, it is used for a
fascinator (hair ornament).

1. Consider your design. You may be an
   instinctive designer who can just sit down
   at the machine and produce wonderful
   pieces but, if not, just draw a design on
   paper: flowery shapes with big petals work
   well. Don't make the shape too small and
   fiddly or you'll have trouble stitching it. The
   stitching will be free machine satin stitch, so
   bear this in mind. Draw in some areas within
   the shape that could be filled. The stitching
   should be quite heavy as that enables
   manipulation when dissolved. When you are
   happy with the design, lay the water-soluble
   film over the top and draw over the design.

2. Lay the water-soluble film over two layers of
   net, making sure that you have enough for
   the whole piece. Place in a frame and tighten
   as much as possible.

3. Set up your machine for free machine
   stitching with metallic thread on the top
   and on the bobbin too, if your machine is
   happy with this. If not, use a toning thread.
   I like a gold or copper used together with
   a variegated, coloured metallic thread. Now
   begin to stitch, using a straight stitch and
   following the lines of the drawing.

4. Stitch again over the straight stitching with
   satin stitch; 5mm width, tapering to 2mm at
   the top should do the trick. Some machines
   allow you to reduce the width as you stitch
   but don't worry about this as the net makes
   the lines a little blocky anyway.

5. Remove from the frame and add a little
   infill stitching, such as free machine straight
   stitching or a light built-in pattern. Then
   cut out the shape, being careful not to cut
   the stitching. Trimming can be performed
   after dissolving when the film forms a less
   fragile surface.

6. Before dissolving, manipulate the piece by
   folding and pinning to hold the shape in
   place. Long leaves can be rolled and pinned.
   There is no right or wrong – just play with
   the shape until you get a good result. When
   happy, dissolve with the pins in place, holding
   each piece in your hand under running water.
   Test frequently to check that you can feel
   that some of the film remains. It should feel a
   little slimy but will dry to quite a hard surface.
   Leave to dry on non-stick baking paper.

7. Now the fun begins: put it all together,
   perhaps nesting flowers in flowers, adding
   beads or wrapped florists' wire, tightly
   wound around a knitting needle. Finally, stitch
   to a support such as a comb or clip.

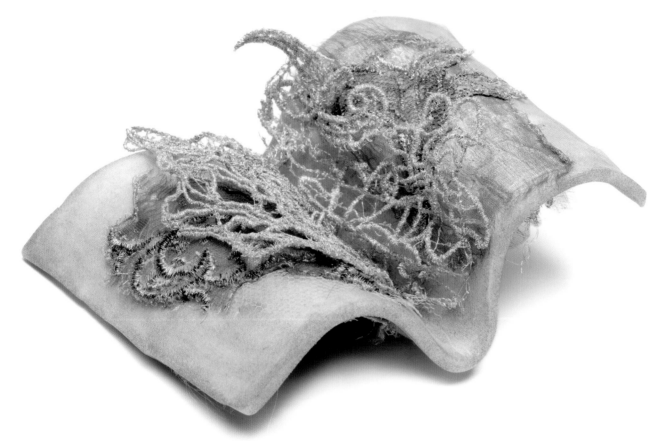

The net motifs could be further enhanced by using an almost dry paintbrush with a little acrylic paint and then sprinkling with embossing powder. Use a heat tool when dry.

∧ *This 'book' is formed from mouldable foam (Softsculpt) with the leaves made from machined florists' wire.*

∨ *Detail of the Softsculpt book showing how stitched net was lightly dusted with embossing powder.*

Water-soluble film and fibres

The idea here is to trap fibres between two layers of soluble fabric and then stitch the resulting sandwich to trap them within a web of stitch.

> Trapped fibres before stitching.

∨ 'Bird Vessel' by Lesley Irving. Lesley has produced this lovely piece of work, using the trapped silk method. The fabric has been formed into a large vessel and enhanced by the addition of the birds, stitched as slips and applied.

Trapped silk fibres

A lighter-weight film can be used here and the more fabric-like solubles are also effective. A little of the film can remain in the fibres, which makes it an ideal technique for vessels. Fringing effects can easily be created by not stitching the topmost fibres. I've used carded silk here.

The basic technique goes like this:

1. Cut two rectangles of film: they should be the same size. If making a vessel, experiment with newspaper to get the size right but allow for a little shrinkage. Also allow for a top fringe, if required, by drawing a line in the water-soluble film some way from the edge.

2. Lay one rectangle on a work surface and pull out hanks of fibre to lay on top.

3. Just like felt making, place another layer at right-angles and then a final one at right-angles again.

4. Place the remaining rectangle on top and pin securely all around the edges and at several points in the middle, making sure that it is all holding together well. Purists would no doubt wish it to be tacked in rows but I find this method works fine.

∧ The vessel shown here was made by stitching silk with water-soluble film. After dissolving, the fabric was stitched with an overlay of dissolved stitching. It was then sprayed with water to dampen it and formed around a jar. The seam was slip stitched, and an overlay applied.

5. Now stitch in a random fashion (or using a grid if the fancy takes you), keeping the meandering lines of stitching overlapping to form pockets to hold the fibre. Don't forget to leave the fringe area free from stitching. Remove the pins as you come to them.

6. Dissolve the film by placing in a bowl and gently running water over the top. Leave a little film in place for a vessel.

7. Wrap around a bottle or suitable shape to dry.

The fringe will have absorbed some of the soluble film and it will probably be sticking up in a 'punky' fashion. You might like this but, if not, wait until it is all dry, remove from the bottle and turn upside down to soak just the fringe. Dry with the fringe at the bottom and tease out when dry, then secure the seam. These vessels look great with an overlay over the top. They also work as flat pieces with added fabric scraps.

∧ *This piece was made using the trapped silk method. Scraps of lace and scrim were added before stitching.*

Trilobal nylon fibres

These are made from synthetic fibres that react to heat. They can be trapped in water-soluble film and stitched, exactly as the silk was, but the trick here is to zap the piece with a heat tool when it has been dissolved and is quite dry. Use a cotton or metallic thread – rayon is not good as it might disappear in the heat. The stitching makes a lot of difference – heavy stitching inhibits the zapping and allows more of the fibre to remain. Both heavy and light stitching work well, so it depends on the effect you want to achieve. Very light stitching can produce wonderful, wispy gossamer pieces. Do lots of samples, trying different stitch densities and all kinds of thread.

The piece shown here used free machined straight stitching in a fairly random fashion, together with the odd area of heavier stitching (built-in patterns) as a contrast. You can see from the result that the more heavily stitched areas have retained the fibres and are therefore more dense and colourful.

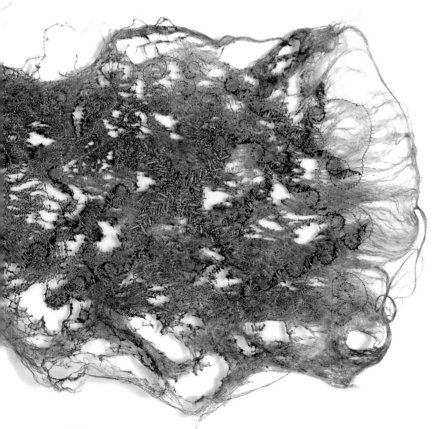

< *This sample was made from trilobal nylon fibres trapped between layers of water-soluble film. Heavy stitching, using metallic thread and the machine's built-in patterns, holds it together. After dissolving, the piece was zapped with a heat tool to distress the nylon fibres and leave the stitching intact.*

SECTION 3:
Creative Conclusions

This section mixes up and extends some of the materials and techniques from Sections 1 and 2, suggesting a more experimental approach. Greater use is made of water-soluble paper, with some more unusual materials added for mixed media effects. Even the humble plastic bag can be used and fallen leaves make great moulds for dissolvable paper casts. Techniques such as rusting, embossing and painting give effects that translate to book covers and wall panels.

Cast paper embellishments

Water-soluble paper can be used with stamps, blocks or even leaves to form perfect casts. Because the paper is designed to dissolve, it takes a more precise impression than the usual pulp. I have covered this technique in other books but we will be using it here in a different way. For those who have missed it, here is the basic technique.

1. Take a wooden block or deeply etched rubber stamp.

2. Tear the water-soluble paper into postage stamp-sized pieces and place in layers on the block or stamp. Dip a paintbrush into water and slosh on the torn pieces until the paper turns to pulp.

3. When it ceases to look like paper, press into the block or stamp – the water-soluble paper should be quite thick. Dry thoroughly – this may take some time.

4. When dry, remove from the block or stamp. It should come off easily but if not, lift the edges with a darning needle or scissors.

These pieces are useful in their own right but can be very exciting as embellishments as they can be merged so completely into a surface that they look as though they have been carved. They look really good on a paper or card surface.

To integrate, just take a dry surface and place the water-soluble cast in position. Glue in place and then wet the cast shape around the edges with a small paintbrush and use your fingers to squash it completely into the surface. Paint with acrylic paint or acrylic varnish to seal.

< *When dry, the paper will fall quickly off a stamp but a deep block may need the application of scissors to remove it from the cast.*

∧ *Look around for other surfaces suitable for casting. This garden hook is great for producing well-shaped leaves.*

∨ *The cast paper leaves from the block (left), have been applied to a card surface.*

Cast paper on plastic

Try this on black plastic rubbish bags by cutting out a piece of the plastic and stitching it to a background fabric. Then spray it with Moonshadow Mist or a similar metallic spray. For some reason, this adheres to the plastic really well, but do try small samples of whatever metallic sprays you have. It does seem to vary with different plastic bags, so try some samples as you don't want it flaking off after the piece is finished. If the spray doesn't work, just use wax or Markal afterwards. Then lay on pieces of fine metal shim and painted cast paper, some very flat, some raised; allow some of the plastic to show. Stitch them down, using a strong shape or shapes as a focal point.

∧ This plastic bin liner has been stitched to a firm fabric and then sprayed with paint. Coloured metallic wax works really well on this surface.

< Impress Me Now have good stamps for focal points. These figures were cast on different sizes of stamp with water-soluble paper. Further casts came from an old box. I really like the subtle gleam from the bin liner.

Kozo fibres

Water-soluble paper works well with the addition of kozo fibres to add texture.

Kozo is a dried, bark-like fibre, often used to make paper. It does, however, have important properties for anyone who loves stitching and mixed media. If the coarse fibres are soaked in cold water so that they soften, they can be teased out gently into magical shapes or formed into a lattice-like structure which can support further embellishment. It's an addictive process but, luckily, kozo is not expensive. Here's how:

1. Pull or cut some thick strands from the kozo and leave to soak for an hour. Then remove from the bowl, blot and leave to dry just a little.

2. Now cut or pull a strand from one of the lengths and gently pull it apart. Shape it into flowers and trees, leaves or abstract shapes. Place a small piece of water-soluble paper on baking paper and dissolve it a little. Try setting the kozo into the pulp and allow to dry.

3. While wet, introduce a little runny paint to the pulp and just touch with a loaded paintbrush (you could also paint with acrylics when dry).

That's just one idea – great for a card or as the centre of a tiny, precious embroidery.

> *This small kozo sample suggested the shape of a tree. A little colour was added while the pulp was wet and the tree shape was given greater definition by rubbing the surface with a dark grey crayon when the paper was dry.*

∧ This kozo landscape
had a small amount of
gesso added in places for
texture. It was painted
in pale colours for a
dreamy effect before a
tiny amount of dissolved
pattern was added to
define a single area
and take the eye into
the distance.

Landscape with kozo fibres

This is another technique that embraces the ability of kozo to resemble natural forms. It can be extended in many ways and I'm sure you will think of lots more. The addition of kozo fibres to water-soluble paper makes it very tough and it can be formed into shapes.

1. Before you begin, soak some kozo fibres for about an hour so that they become pliable.

2. Lay a double piece of water-soluble paper on a sheet of non-stick baking paper. Dissolve, using water on a paintbrush; allow some holes to develop. Pull the kozo fibres apart, as before, and add to the paper, embedding it in the pulp.

3. Pull more kozo fibres apart. Make some large shapes for foreground trees, small shapes for distant clumps of trees and straight spiky shapes for foreground grasses.

4. Place the kozo shapes on top of the dissolved paper, pressing them well into the mush. Add dry pieces of water-soluble paper over the top in some places and work them with your finger until they are absorbed and mushy. Slightly coat the kozo like this in places. In others, leave it on top but well embedded in the pulp.

5. When almost dry, form into a shape like the one in my landscape piece. If dry enough, it will hold the shape. Then dry completely.

6. When dry, brush with gesso – lightly in some places, heavily in others. If I decide to have only a hint of colour, I usually spray with a little runny paint at this stage. It will absorb into the surface. It is possible to add deeper colour to trees and foreground grasses by putting some silk paint (or similar) on a brush and painting them with a very light touch. If you are too heavy-handed, spray with water or add more gesso.

7. Finally, add stitch if you wish or apply cast paper by the 'dissolving in' method. Small pieces of stitching previously worked on water-soluble film can also be useful but don't add too much embellishment – let the kozo take centre stage.

> Here you can see the water-soluble and kozo fibres formed into a suitable shape for a three-dimensional landscape. It is now ready to dry.

∨ A plastic bag background supports areas of water-soluble paper and kozo fibre. The central area of embossed shim is surrounded by embossing powder on felt. The moulding mat stamp used squashed the melted UTEE into interesting shapes which were then cut out and applied by stitching into the felt backing.

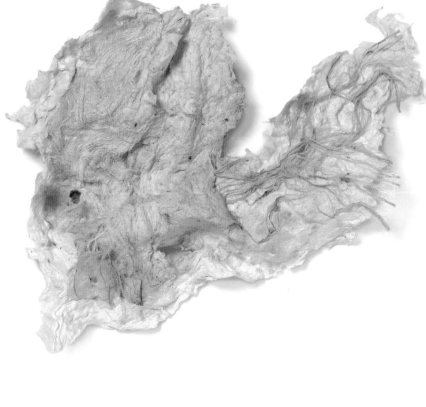

Extension technique

The landscape idea could be used in other ways. Here is one idea:

1. Use a suitable backing – heavy Vilene or felt (felt takes a long time to dry). Plastic bin liner could look good, too.

2. Lay pieces of water-soluble paper on the background. Some of them could be stamped with Xpandaprint first and puffed with a heat tool. Stitch lightly around the edges, using a zigzag or open pattern.

3. Add some metal shim – stitch to the base. Perhaps build up heavily stitched pieces of water-soluble film which has been dissolved and dried. Try laying these over the metal.

4. Dissolve with water on a paintbrush, adding a little kozo. Dry.

5. Brush with gesso, lightly in some places, heavily in others.

6. Paint when dry, or spray with fountain-pen ink, which turns a lovely blue-grey.

Water-soluble paper layers

I am always very taken by distressed surfaces, particularly rusted ones, and layers of treated water-soluble paper can produce a wonderful rusted effect. I'm not going to go step-by-step through the making, but overleaf are some ideas for the layers.

∨ *Here layers of water-soluble paper, some rusted, are interspersed with wrapped pipe cleaners. The background to which they are stitched is tea-dyed tissue paper on craft Vilene.*

Rust effects

These can be achieved in many ways. Sometimes, just painting layers of water-soluble paper in suitable colours can give a rusted effect.

① Rusting powder

Rusting powder will give even greater degrees of rust and it sticks well to resists that will stop all the paper washing away. To do this, paint or stamp onto the soluble paper. You can use a variety of media from paint and puff paint to acrylic gels. Sprinkle with rusting powder and then spray with water which will dissolve some of the paper. The rusty puffed bit will resist the water and is ready for a spray of white vinegar to hasten the rusting process. Other vinegars will work but are a bit smelly, as you cannot wash it out.

② Ink and bleach

Bear in mind that most fountain-pen inks react to bleach by turning rusty orange. Try dissolving some water-soluble paper on a metallic mesh, such as Wiremesh. Paint with ink while pulpy and then bleach when dry. Add acrylic paints in greens and rusty colours. The mesh can be manipulated into shapes and folds when dry.

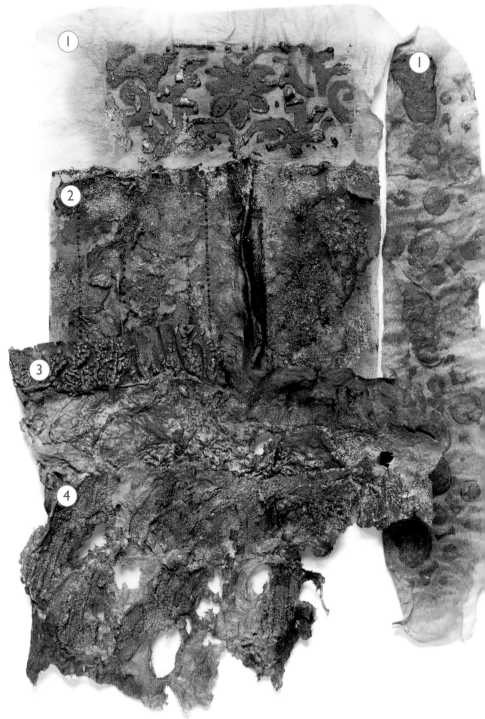

③ Puff paint

I find that puff paint, such as Xpandaprint, works really well. Just stamp or paint on the water-soluble paper, perhaps drawing an old needle through the puff paint to make marks, as in the border shown here. Then puff and paint with acrylics in rusty oranges. While the paint is wet, sprinkle with rust-coloured embossing powder (the ordinary one, not UTEE) and puff. It is also possible to do this in reverse by sprinkling the embossing powder into the puff paint, before heating.

④ Puff paint and embossing powder

Rust-coloured embossing powder can be found by Googling – or you might try Ranger's Tim Holtz distressed embossing powder – the mahogany is good for a rusty look. It is great on water-soluble paper which can be dissolved, as before, and painted with metallic paints.

A great effect, suitable for sketchbooks, can be achieved by using a large stamp or block with puff paint. Print the paint onto two layers of water-soluble paper and then sprinkle rusty-coloured embossing powder onto it. Puff and dissolve. Then use the same stamp directly onto the page, using puff paint and rusty embossing powder as before. When the water-soluble is dry, tear off fragments and stick over the stamp on the sketchbook page, lining up the pattern so that it matches. Paint the entire piece when dry.

> Sketchbook page with rusty-coloured embossing powders. The raised area is embossed water-soluble paper impressed with the same stamp.

This photo, right, of an old rusty plane, really gave me a great starting point for a piece of work. It was rotated to give a better shape.

Kozo could be added to any of these pieces as it gives so much strength to the dissolved paper.

When you have a few sheets of rusted, puffed, embossed and generally distressed paper, paint them with acrylics in suitable colours and dry. Then begin to layer them on top of each other. Tear them, stitch them and fiddle with them until they look like a very old, very tatty, rusty surface. Don't overlook the possibility of a little metallic wax, but keep it low-key.

Finally, hand stitch them together using strong thread and a loose stabbing stitch. Arrange according to your design. I built mine up from the base on a piece of craft Vilene. This was huge fun and I hope your piece has worked out just as well.

Well, we seem to have come a long way from our starting point of encrusted surfaces. I hope the book has shown you the possibilities inherent in dissolvable media. Use them as a starting point and stretch the techniques, especially the ones in the last section. Must go, as I'm off to work some trilobal nylon and Lutradur into the rusty bits; just think of all that distressing with a bit of zapping added to the mix!

> This piece was based on the photograph of a rusty old plane. The design worked best when rotated to the right. It was stitched on Vilene and then applied to a stretcher which had been treated with rusting powder. It makes a useful sampler, showing all the rusting methods.